CONTACT INFORMATION
NAME	
PHONE #	
ADDRESS	
EMAIL	

Copyright © Teresa Rother
All rights reserved. No part of this publication may be reproduced, distributed, or transmitted in any form or by any means, including photocopy, recording, or other electronic or mechanical methods.

DEDICATION

This Vehicle Maintenance Book is dedicated to all the people who want to track and record the maintenance and upkeep of their vehicles.

You are my inspiration for producing this book and I'm honored to be a part of your record-keeping and organization.

HOW TO USE THIS BOOK

This Vehicle Maintenance Book will help you by accurately recording each repair, service maintenance updates, as well as fuel and mileage for road trips.

Here are examples of information for you to fill in and write the details of your logbook.

Fill in the following information:

1. Contact List- write down contacts for mechanics, local DMV, auto insurance company, and more
2. Maintenance- Log date, serviced by, odometer reading, details, cost
3. Repairs- record date, serviced by, details, cost
4. Fuel Log- record date, odometer reading, MPG/KMPL, station
5. Trip Log- record date, odometer reading (beginning and end), distance, hours, destination or purpose, business expense (fuel, tolls, parking, other)

CONTACT LIST

NAME	CONTACT INFORMATION

MAINTENANCE - JANUARY

DATE	SERVICED BY	ODOMETER READING	DETAILS	COST

REPAIRS - JANUARY

DATE	SERVICED BY	DETAILS	COST

FUEL LOG - JANUARY

DATE	ODOMETER READING	GAS/LITERS	COST	MPG/KMPL	STATION

TRIP LOG- JANUARY

DATE	ODOMETER READING		DISTANCE	HOURS	DESTINATION OR PURPOSE	BUSINESS EXPENSE			
	BEGIN	END				FUEL	TOLLS	PARKING	OTHER

MAINTENANCE- FEBRUARY

DATE	SERVICED BY	ODOMETER READING	DETAILS	COST

REPAIRS- FEBRUARY

DATE	SERVICED BY	DETAILS	COST

FUEL LOG - FEBRUARY

DATE	ODOMETER READING	GAS/LITERS	COST	MPG/KMPL	STATION

TRIP LOG - FEBRUARY

DATE	ODOMETER READING		DISTANCE	HOURS	DESTINATION OR PURPOSE	BUSINESS EXPENSE			
	BEGIN	END				FUEL	TOLLS	PARKING	OTHER

MAINTENANCE- MARCH

DATE	SERVICED BY	ODOMETER READING	DETAILS	COST

REPAIRS- MARCH

DATE	SERVICED BY	DETAILS	COST

FUEL LOG - MARCH

DATE	ODOMETER READING	GAS/LITERS	COST	MPG/KMPL	STATION

TRIP LOG - MARCH

DATE	ODOMETER READING		DISTANCE	HOURS	DESTINATION OR PURPOSE	BUSINESS EXPENSE			
	BEGIN	END				FUEL	TOLLS	PARKING	OTHER

MAINTENANCE- APRIL

DATE	SERVICED BY	ODOMETER READING	DETAILS	COST

REPAIRS- APRIL

DATE	SERVICED BY	DETAILS	COST

FUEL LOG- APRIL

DATE	ODOMETER READING	GAS/LITERS	COST	MPG/KMPL	STATION

TRIP LOG- APRIL

DATE	ODOMETER READING		DISTANCE	HOURS	DESTINATION OR PURPOSE	BUSINESS EXPENSE			
	BEGIN	END				FUEL	TOLLS	PARKING	OTHER

MAINTENANCE- MAY

DATE	SERVICED BY	ODOMETER READING	DETAILS	COST

REPAIRS- MAY

DATE	SERVICED BY	DETAILS	COST

FUEL LOG - MAY

DATE	ODOMETER READING	GAS/LITERS	COST	MPG/KMPL	STATION

TRIP LOG- MAY

DATE	ODOMETER READING		DISTANCE	HOURS	DESTINATION OR PURPOSE	BUSINESS EXPENSE			
	BEGIN	END				FUEL	TOLLS	PARKING	OTHER

MAINTENANCE- JUNE

DATE	SERVICED BY	ODOMETER READING	DETAILS	COST

REPAIRS- JUNE

DATE	SERVICED BY	DETAILS	COST

FUEL LOG - JUNE

DATE	ODOMETER READING	GAS/LITERS	COST	MPG/KMPL	STATION

TRIP LOG- JUNE

DATE	ODOMETER READING		DISTANCE	HOURS	DESTINATION OR PURPOSE	BUSINESS EXPENSE			
	BEGIN	END				FUEL	TOLLS	PARKING	OTHER

MAINTENANCE - JULY

DATE	SERVICED BY	ODOMETER READING	DETAILS	COST

REPAIRS- JULY

DATE	SERVICED BY	DETAILS	COST

FUEL LOG - JULY

DATE	ODOMETER READING	GAS/LITERS	COST	MPG/KMPL	STATION

TRIP LOG - JULY

DATE	ODOMETER READING		DISTANCE	HOURS	DESTINATION OR PURPOSE	BUSINESS EXPENSE			
	BEGIN	END				FUEL	TOLLS	PARKING	OTHER

MAINTENANCE- AUGUST

DATE	SERVICED BY	ODOMETER READING	DETAILS	COST

REPAIRS- AUGUST

DATE	SERVICED BY	DETAILS	COST

FUEL LOG- AUGUST

DATE	ODOMETER READING	GAS/LITERS	COST	MPG/KMPL	STATION

TRIP LOG- AUGUST

DATE	ODOMETER READING		DISTANCE	HOURS	DESTINATION OR PURPOSE	BUSINESS EXPENSE			
	BEGIN	END				FUEL	TOLLS	PARKING	OTHER

MAINTENANCE - SEPTEMBER

DATE	SERVICED BY	ODOMETER READING	DETAILS	COST

REPAIRS- SEPTEMBER

DATE	SERVICED BY	DETAILS	COST

FUEL LOG - SEPTEMBER

DATE	ODOMETER READING	GAS/LITERS	COST	MPG/KMPL	STATION

TRIP LOG- SEPTEMBER

DATE	ODOMETER READING		DISTANCE	HOURS	DESTINATION OR PURPOSE	BUSINESS EXPENSE			
	BEGIN	END				FUEL	TOLLS	PARKING	OTHER

MAINTENANCE - OCTOBER

DATE	SERVICED BY	ODOMETER READING	DETAILS	COST

REPAIRS- OCTOBER

DATE	SERVICED BY	DETAILS	COST

FUEL LOG - OCTOBER

DATE	ODOMETER READING	GAS/LITERS	COST	MPG/KMPL	STATION

TRIP LOG- OCTOBER

DATE	ODOMETER READING		DISTANCE	HOURS	DESTINATION OR PURPOSE	BUSINESS EXPENSE			
	BEGIN	END				FUEL	TOLLS	PARKING	OTHER

MAINTENANCE - NOVEMBER

DATE	SERVICED BY	ODOMETER READING	DETAILS	COST

REPAIRS- NOVEMBER

DATE	SERVICED BY	DETAILS	COST

FUEL LOG - NOVEMBER

DATE	ODOMETER READING	GAS/LITERS	COST	MPG/KMPL	STATION

TRIP LOG- NOVEMBER

DATE	ODOMETER READING		DISTANCE	HOURS	DESTINATION OR PURPOSE	BUSINESS EXPENSE			
	BEGIN	END				FUEL	TOLLS	PARKING	OTHER

MAINTENANCE- DECEMBER

DATE	SERVICED BY	ODOMETER READING	DETAILS	COST

REPAIRS- DECEMBER

DATE	SERVICED BY	DETAILS	COST

FUEL LOG- DECEMBER

DATE	ODOMETER READING	GAS/LITERS	COST	MPG/KMPL	STATION

TRIP LOG- DECEMBER

DATE	ODOMETER READING		DISTANCE	HOURS	DESTINATION OR PURPOSE	BUSINESS EXPENSE			
	BEGIN	END				FUEL	TOLLS	PARKING	OTHER

YEARLY SUMMARY

MONTH	TOTAL DISTANCE	TOTAL COST OF FUEL	TOTAL REPAIRS	TOTAL MAINT.	TOTAL REPAIRS
JANUARY					
FEBRUARY					
MARCH					
APRIL					
MAY					
JUNE					

NOTES

YEARLY SUMMARY

MONTH	TOTAL DISTANCE	TOTAL COST OF FUEL	TOTAL REPAIRS	TOTAL MAINT.	TOTAL REPAIRS
JULY					
AUGUST					
SEPTEMBER					
OCTOBER					
NOVEMBER					
DECEMBER					

NOTES

MAINTENANCE- JANUARY

DATE	SERVICED BY	ODOMETER READING	DETAILS	COST

REPAIRS - JANUARY

DATE	SERVICED BY	DETAILS	COST

FUEL LOG - JANUARY

DATE	ODOMETER READING	GAS/LITERS	COST	MPG/KMPL	STATION

TRIP LOG- JANUARY

DATE	ODOMETER READING		DISTANCE	HOURS	DESTINATION OR PURPOSE	BUSINESS EXPENSE			
	BEGIN	END				FUEL	TOLLS	PARKING	OTHER

MAINTENANCE - FEBRUARY

DATE	SERVICED BY	ODOMETER READING	DETAILS	COST

REPAIRS- FEBRUARY

DATE	SERVICED BY	DETAILS	COST

FUEL LOG - FEBRUARY

DATE	ODOMETER READING	GAS/LITERS	COST	MPG/KMPL	STATION

TRIP LOG- FEBRUARY

DATE	ODOMETER READING		DISTANCE	HOURS	DESTINATION OR PURPOSE	BUSINESS EXPENSE			
	BEGIN	END				FUEL	TOLLS	PARKING	OTHER

MAINTENANCE- MARCH

DATE	SERVICED BY	ODOMETER READING	DETAILS	COST

REPAIRS- MARCH

DATE	SERVICED BY	DETAILS	COST

FUEL LOG - MARCH

DATE	ODOMETER READING	GAS/LITERS	COST	MPG/KMPL	STATION

TRIP LOG - MARCH

DATE	ODOMETER READING		DISTANCE	HOURS	DESTINATION OR PURPOSE	BUSINESS EXPENSE			
	BEGIN	END				FUEL	TOLLS	PARKING	OTHER

MAINTENANCE - APRIL

DATE	SERVICED BY	ODOMETER READING	DETAILS	COST

REPAIRS- APRIL

DATE	SERVICED BY	DETAILS	COST

FUEL LOG- APRIL

DATE	ODOMETER READING	GAS/LITERS	COST	MPG/KMPL	STATION

TRIP LOG- APRIL

DATE	ODOMETER READING		DISTANCE	HOURS	DESTINATION OR PURPOSE	BUSINESS EXPENSE			
	BEGIN	END				FUEL	TOLLS	PARKING	OTHER

MAINTENANCE- MAY

DATE	SERVICED BY	ODOMETER READING	DETAILS	COST

REPAIRS- MAY

DATE	SERVICED BY	DETAILS	COST

FUEL LOG- MAY

DATE	ODOMETER READING	GAS/LITERS	COST	MPG/KMPL	STATION

TRIP LOG- MAY

DATE	ODOMETER READING		DISTANCE	HOURS	DESTINATION OR PURPOSE	BUSINESS EXPENSE			
	BEGIN	END				FUEL	TOLLS	PARKING	OTHER

MAINTENANCE- JUNE

DATE	SERVICED BY	ODOMETER READING	DETAILS	COST

REPAIRS- JUNE

DATE	SERVICED BY	DETAILS	COST

FUEL LOG- JUNE

DATE	ODOMETER READING	GAS/LITERS	COST	MPG/KMPL	STATION

TRIP LOG - JUNE

DATE	ODOMETER READING		DISTANCE	HOURS	DESTINATION OR PURPOSE	BUSINESS EXPENSE			
	BEGIN	END				FUEL	TOLLS	PARKING	OTHER

MAINTENANCE - JULY

DATE	SERVICED BY	ODOMETER READING	DETAILS	COST

REPAIRS- JULY

DATE	SERVICED BY	DETAILS	COST

FUEL LOG - JULY

DATE	ODOMETER READING	GAS/LITERS	COST	MPG/KMPL	STATION

TRIP LOG - JULY

DATE	ODOMETER READING		DISTANCE	HOURS	DESTINATION OR PURPOSE	BUSINESS EXPENSE			
	BEGIN	END				FUEL	TOLLS	PARKING	OTHER

MAINTENANCE- AUGUST

DATE	SERVICED BY	ODOMETER READING	DETAILS	COST

REPAIRS- AUGUST

DATE	SERVICED BY	DETAILS	COST

FUEL LOG- AUGUST

DATE	ODOMETER READING	GAS/LITERS	COST	MPG/KMPL	STATION

TRIP LOG- AUGUST

DATE	ODOMETER READING		DISTANCE	HOURS	DESTINATION OR PURPOSE	BUSINESS EXPENSE			
	BEGIN	END				FUEL	TOLLS	PARKING	OTHER

MAINTENANCE- SEPTEMBER

DATE	SERVICED BY	ODOMETER READING	DETAILS	COST

REPAIRS- SEPTEMBER

DATE	SERVICED BY	DETAILS	COST

FUEL LOG - SEPTEMBER

DATE	ODOMETER READING	GAS/LITERS	COST	MPG/KMPL	STATION

TRIP LOG - SEPTEMBER

DATE	ODOMETER READING		DISTANCE	HOURS	DESTINATION OR PURPOSE	BUSINESS EXPENSE			
	BEGIN	END				FUEL	TOLLS	PARKING	OTHER

MAINTENANCE - OCTOBER

DATE	SERVICED BY	ODOMETER READING	DETAILS	COST

REPAIRS- OCTOBER

DATE	SERVICED BY	DETAILS	COST

FUEL LOG - OCTOBER

DATE	ODOMETER READING	GAS/LITERS	COST	MPG/KMPL	STATION

TRIP LOG - OCTOBER

DATE	ODOMETER READING		DISTANCE	HOURS	DESTINATION OR PURPOSE	BUSINESS EXPENSE			
	BEGIN	END				FUEL	TOLLS	PARKING	OTHER

MAINTENANCE - NOVEMBER

DATE	SERVICED BY	ODOMETER READING	DETAILS	COST

REPAIRS- NOVEMBER

DATE	SERVICED BY	DETAILS	COST

FUEL LOG- NOVEMBER

DATE	ODOMETER READING	GAS/LITERS	COST	MPG/KMPL	STATION

TRIP LOG - NOVEMBER

DATE	ODOMETER READING		DISTANCE	HOURS	DESTINATION OR PURPOSE	BUSINESS EXPENSE			
	BEGIN	END				FUEL	TOLLS	PARKING	OTHER

MAINTENANCE- DECEMBER

DATE	SERVICED BY	ODOMETER READING	DETAILS	COST

REPAIRS- DECEMBER

DATE	SERVICED BY	DETAILS	COST

FUEL LOG- DECEMBER

DATE	ODOMETER READING	GAS/LITERS	COST	MPG/KMPL	STATION

TRIP LOG- DECEMBER

DATE	ODOMETER READING		DISTANCE	HOURS	DESTINATION OR PURPOSE	BUSINESS EXPENSE			
	BEGIN	END				FUEL	TOLLS	PARKING	OTHER

YEARLY SUMMARY

MONTH	TOTAL DISTANCE	TOTAL COST OF FUEL	TOTAL REPAIRS	TOTAL MAINT.	TOTAL REPAIRS
JANUARY					
FEBRUARY					
MARCH					
APRIL					
MAY					
JUNE					

NOTES

YEARLY SUMMARY

MONTH	TOTAL DISTANCE	TOTAL COST OF FUEL	TOTAL REPAIRS	TOTAL MAINT.	TOTAL REPAIRS
JULY					
AUGUST					
SEPTEMBER					
OCTOBER					
NOVEMBER					
DECEMBER					

NOTES

www.ingramcontent.com/pod-product-compliance
Lightning Source LLC
Chambersburg PA
CBHW071251070526
44583CB00017B/2418